Lord Rooker's Requiem 38

Lounge 39

Man and Machine 40

Mobile Stones 42

Monitor 43

Motherhood is a Rhinoceros 44

Mrs Meacher 45

My Foolish Lover Gave Me Chocolates.......................................46

The New Zoo 47

Pentad...48

Picking My Nose 49

Proud...50

Rose...51

Rowner in the Rain..52

Sexting 54

Smoke Me 55

Snow Castles...56

The Sun on the Other Side 58

The Time of Your Life 59

Wacko Jacko 60

The Way I Want to Go 61

Words Like Needles 62

You Wake 63

Zoo Villanelle 64

Contents

Afterlife...5

The Argentine 6

Axe..8

Bête Noire...10

Bet Your Life..12

Bubbles 13

Carriwitchet 14

Cricket Widow..15

Dante's Road 16

Day at the Bitch 17

DC Dreaming..18

Earthling..19

The English Woman 20

Fanny Farts 21

Feel the Difference 22

Fiction and Fingerprints 23

Fields of Dorset - Jackalents 24

Four Ladies 25

Guga..26

Gwen...28

How to Speak to Lions 29

Hygiene..30

Instinct...31

John & Gwen 32

The Journey of the Ants 33

The Last Room 34

Lawnmower 35

Lazy Day at the Fete..36

Leviathan 37

Afterlife

Snippets of solitude outside the memory
of people who whisper fragments
do not form part of my afterlife.

My presence is preserved in garments,
in old photographs, associated events;
a wedding, christening, Christmas clothes;

errors of judgement more remembered
than small acts of triumph,
averted catastrophes or daily duty.

Some grandchild's feature may disturb
a thought of the way the light reflects
my eyes, some expression, some phrase

written, opinions as the evidence
I am, was, here; strangeness, estrangement
argument with those too similar, too different.

How each acquaintance can hold a moment
of my apprenticeship, a strand
to be woven in caricature of my existence.

The Argentine

The dust plumes from the gaucho's Stetson
as he shakes off the ride across the Pampas.
He sees the promise beneath the sheath skirt,
the curve of her mouth under carmine tint.

She circles him, assessing the invitation to dance.
Her nose nestles against his cheek then turns,
disdaining the stench of his work.
Her hands caress hungrily for signs of wealth*

On the lurid dance floor she bends to his lead.
Light catches their embrace, their sway, their walk,
She turns to left, to right in figures of eight
each time her calf sweeps, feathering his shin.

He strides outside her steps, his feet
trick and trespass between her ankles.
Her glissade halts in rapid flicks, he copies
and they pirouette in arpeggio precision.

She twists against his hold, aware she is falling.
He catches her arm and pulls her to him,
makes barriers† to her escape, chases her retreat,
lifts her easily as a puppeteer his marionette.

Their bodies move in legato structures, as one,
as the habañera rhythm leads them into fugue,
abandoning solitude in the undulating dance.
The music stops. Negotiations are complete.

*The dancer wants to make sure the gaucho's wallet is full, that he's
been paid.
†Tango steps: Abrazo – embrace, Caminar – walk, Giros – turns,
Contragiros – counter-turns, Ochos – figures of eight, Barridas–
barriers, Cozas – chases and Ganchos – leg hooks. The poem uses
anglicized descriptions for these specific movements.

Axe

No one prepares you for the guilt
over every choice
the nappy, the food, the clothes;
even if you wanted green for your girl,
all you can buy is pink.
Terry nappies are ecological
except for all the detergent,
fossil fuel used to run the washing machine.
God forbid you do it by hand;
up to your forearms in mustard.
Pampers clog the land-fill sites –
just let the beast dangle
over the loo at incontinent moments.
Then breast or bottle arguments,
a dozen midwives
handling your breasts
like so much chopped liver,
without a by-your-leave,
to force a nipple
into sproglet lips.

Should you work;
time spent away, missed events –
like the first step –
the nursery deny she's been walking
for a week
to make you think you saw
the first step and can thrill about it
like stay-at-home mothers;
ones prepared with wet-wipes, toys,
feed supplies and a change of clothes.

Should your child wield an axe
to mutilate their victim,
everyone assumes it's the mother's fault.

Bête Noire

Moods that sink me beyond control
worse than trauma, much worse by far;
chance or purpose that harms my child.
C'est juste ma bête noire

When the darkness comes like a hound
hunting prey. That despondent cur
wails his mournful, unending song.
C'est juste ma bête bleu

When I'm craven and Hobson weak,
when I'm facing the threats alone
flight is choice for this timid deer.
C'est juste ma bête jaune.

Shrew-like temper at sexist slurs,
boiling blood in a hot deluge
flows unleashed at the hapless man.
C'est juste ma bête rouge.

Lays in wait like a cuckoo's chick;
doubt, mistrust in what lovers share,
suspicion in the nest we built.
C'est juste ma bête verte.

Noble duty; I'm one to call,
full of virtue, my morals staunch.
Self righteous as a Seraph saint.
C'est juste ma bête blanche.

Flights of fantasy, elusive
butterflies in a hidden grove
yield to dreams of a peaceful world.
C'est juste ma bête mauve.

Given time as a healer, hope
crawls out, sluggish over the lows,
lenses tint and my tankard fills
C'est juste ma bête rose.

Bet Your Life

Mary sat across from Peter. Their pills
were strewn like smarties, ready for the kill.
Some gamblers bet on who'd be first to leave
but rareness won like aces up your sleeve.
First Mary lead with stroke and Pete with gout
then Mary's teeth came loose; she took them out.
But Peter laid an eyeball, upped the stakes,
so Mary countered with the drugs she takes
for her transplanted kidney. Pete thought quick;
the chemo stuff that stopped him being sick.
She weakened when she bet her diarrhoea.
The gallant Pete gave soothing panacea;
the lozenge looking tablet - cobalt blue -
prolonged their romance for a year or two.

Bubbles

The toy shop sets a child snare;
a battery operated blowing machine
shaping souped-up liquid into streams
of pinkish orbs across the thoroughfare.
A grandpa watches his little charge;
merino tufts escaping from a baseball cap
and turned out smartly by *Kids at Gap*,
on tip toe to capture the globes at large.
A bubble settles on the boy's sleeve
and stays there for the briefest stand.
It vanishes when grandpa takes his hand,
'Come on lad, it's time to leave.'
The boy reluctantly stops chasing the foam
and asks, 'Can we take some of them home?'

Carriwitchet

To give your words a modern slant
use slang like arrows, loud and fouth.
For those who can and those who cant
to pramp your words into their mouths

use slang like arrows, loud and fouth;
jawbreakers fit to water eyes
and pramp your words into their mouths.
Seek truth or where you hope it lies,

jawbreakers fit to water eyes
and sounds as grounded heel and sole.
Seek truth or where you hope it lies
with words that tear and take a toll

and soundly ground to heal a soul
to sing of love or make them laugh.
The words that tear and take a toll
with pithy neoteric craft

to sing of love and make them laugh.
For those who can and those who cant
use pithy neoteric craft
to give your words a modern slant.

Cricket Widow

I sat in the car with a picnic,
reading a book and sipping wine.
I was supposed to be watching
the men in white
but was engrossed
and I missed
the sixer, till it battered the roof.

Dante's Road

God watches a driver sloshing back coffee
in his 'clean-me' van who tosses a still
lit cigarette stub on my bonnet,

eating another Big Mac that the girl
at Welcome Break sold along with the bars
of chocolate that congest his glove box.

God counts the Mercedes badges knowing
how I dream of the lottery win to get one,
with better gadgets than the car in front.

He watches the blue-tooth talker who's
too important to leave the office,
too insecure his portfolio will crash.

God sees the glamour puss pouting for lip gloss
with her hair straighteners plugged in the lighter
socket, unaware that the lane is moving.

She thinks the hoots are the admiration
of a horny man who likes skirts that ride up
when she slides forwards in her Mini.

But it's the throbbing vein in his temple,
enraged by signs that say forty is safe,
that makes him smash her windscreen with a bat.

Day at the Bitch

Aged seven I was good though slightly wounded.
A fond neighbour; she's wondrous, tall and blonde,
offered a trip: a long journey around;
a van so tight enclosed it is no wonder.

The petrol smell, whilst we were travelling,
was galling when the opened vault unveiled
a pool unparalleled of vile marvel:
the ailment revealed; I could not revel.

Ran to the beach and sat far from the bleach,
slouched like a creature bent eating peaches.
Down beat the marching sun we baked beneath.
I climbed a bleak feature: stretched high and reached.

Descend the last crevasse. The day was past.
Redressed in plastered, massive splash of nasty.
The plastic, glass and trash were cast: dispersed.
No one could class that beastly day a blast.

DC Dreaming
3 November 2008

'Yeah, they forgot the names of quarry slaves
who brought the white stone from the South. Big bucks
built it. Green-backs get you in.' 'That just proves
you know jack,' He spat, 'It was built by Micks.'

'It's like the movies; coloured actors setting
precedents; playing presidents with soul.
He looks like Washington.' I said. Him doubting,
'The monument feller?' 'No, Denzel. Fool.'

'You're dreaming bitch. Them triple K's won't sign
their cross for him.' 'He'll bring the White House race
to heel with hopeful heart. That Kenyan grin
can't harm his chance.' 'If he gets past police.'
''Ole Luther King be proud a pacifist...'
'Good God, next you'll be singing *free at last*.'

Earthling

A man asked me where I came from and
the stranger played a guessing game
because he'd never met me, I was not a neighbour.
He listed continents, countries and homes;
a house, a palace, a caravan, a tent.
and received some thirty 'Nos'.
He tested me with languages
that made my eardrums dream
of exotic places I would like to see.
He asked to whom I prayed and tried
to define my source by siphoning beliefs
and questioned my parentage;
the ancestry of chromosomes
that ruled out certain climates.
I pointed out the laws of naturalisation
some countries offer immigrants
and took away this argument.
Things learned in life gave him no clues
as I refused to be defined by schooling
when experience is the greatest master
and process of thought and curiosity
mean each of us is our own educator.
He asked me once again where I came from.
I replied, 'Same place as you.'

The English Woman

What can be said about the English woman
whose accent changed to her adopted tongue
but never lost all the vowels of native Odiham
that kept her Sassenach to her neighbours,
though she changed her errands for messages.

She resembled Margaret in her younger years
and wore fine rings and regal hair,
paced, quick march, towards each jewellery shop
unless there was a handbag store close by,
concerned as much for rear view as for face.

She fed us Southerners warm, buttered rowies,
Sunday morning gossip of daughters' lives,
consolation offered and received. On holidays
her visits marked by sports-car-rumble snoring,
to dream, forever, of her Scottish lover's greatcoat.

Fanny Farts

To the dear American, fanny fart might
mean a bottom burp. But this ain't what I mean.
Keister ain't the place I intend to pour praise.
                                    It's more the quim quake.

Pressure builds as squelchiness seals escape. Plunge
lavish length in, burial deep inside, slide
back and forth, the vacuum effect to cause post
                                    coital cunt cough.

During lunging, pockets of air get stuck till
he withdraws and gurgling noises trumpet,
like the Eastern custom to belch a full meal,
                                    forced by a tight fit.

Girls' regard for girth can applaud with muff guff.
Gorging gusset sounding the pussy parp stress.
Thunderclap the wonderful width; the whole hole's
                                    rippling fanfare.

Bodies all have ways to express excess wind.
Whoopee cushion winkies are loud and clear, mere
suction function ain't to be blushing beetroot;
                                    welcome the size prize.

Feel the Difference

Breasts impressed with touch of a button thumbprints,
diamond facet quality prows the headlamps,
automatic suspension, pert dual clutch
                                 toggle display switch.

Behind red stitched cushions the split rear seatback
folds to show bold beautiful lines and broad spread
torque that's self-levelling when still; on high gloss
                                 piano black heels.

Frontal bumper skirting the driver cockpit;
horizontal, stroking the column, capless
fuelling systems challenging roads you can't help
                                 falling in love with.

With thanks to the 2011 Ford Mondeo brochure.

Fiction and Fingerprints

We love to read the red-tops' tales when packed
with juicy grist a wily journalist
has penned and, though containing little fact,
the lies he risked, to give the yarn a twist,
of who was kissed and high on drugs or pissed.
It is the stuff of style and flimsy hints.
The star has missed the chance to slap his wrist;
no justice when the truth is indistinct.
All that remains, of news, is carbon fingerprints.

Fields of Dorset - Jackalents

Sea-bitter winds crushed their boats ashore,
broken for firewood, augmented with sedge;
rough scrub fragrant, warmed for a while.

They pitched flimsy shelters in February frost
clinging to cropless rock on cliff-edge steeps.
Hostile villagers prevented escape,
wary of Gallic Jacques, suspect knaves, Huguenots.
Hunger bit deepest through berryless March.

Pestilence took them before the feast day,
masked villagers buried their bones;
hid their ignorance under Jurassic markers.

Four Ladies

At table four, watched by a snail,
four ladies sat, all British pale.
In Spain they drank and bathed in sun.
It's one for all and all for one.
Four ladies sat with dregs of wine
and smiled for José, ass divine
in tight black trousers, served the meal
and dodged the hands that tried to feel.
Away on fun, their bellies full,
four ladies laughed, out on the pull.
No kids, no spouse, no boss, no chores –
no doubt what God made ladies for.

A sisterhood for forty years,
four ladies hide their deepest fears;
one lady's curse to do good deeds,
denies her own for family needs;
one lady's melancholy mood
suppresses angst with comfort food;
one lady has her breast cut off -
the cancer stems her partner's love;
one lady mourns the son who died
and drinks away her loss, and pride.
Four ladies laughter heard no more;
no doubt what God made ladies for.

Los Carracoles (2001).

Guga

To prepare the delicacy
take one stone, granite or gneiss,
place in the pot with the guga,
boil for twenty minutes,
drain the fat and repeat four times.
Add an onion at the fifth boiling.
When the stone softens
the guga is ready to eat.

The guga flesh is fishy duck.
The odour, one could not call it aroma,
is a thousand years of hunting,
a childhood of celebrating
the coastal pabulum.
A cull of chicks, once blue eggs
on Sula Sgeir's razor cliffs
forty miles from human habitation.

Ten men of Ness, foolish or brave
or both, set sail for the nowhere rock.
A tiny bothy is the only shelter,
the monastery derelict, the isle barren
ten months of the year.
Seasick arrival, relief at the landfall
despite the foul stench of gannet guano.
They bring poles, ropes, food and barrels.

The rocks are slick with gizzard,
neck-cracked guga are plucked,
piled in circles of curing salt;
grey carcases like cairns.
The two week ritual leaves no calluses,
but ripped fingers cruciate in brine.
Oilskins offer little warmth
for the bones of Nessmen.

Some sense of perpetuation,
crafts sodality elsewhere abandons,
drives the inexplicable call;
the instinct to return each year
to chance the precipitous cliffs,
proof of life by risking it;
testing brawn, tenacity and species;
a delicacy of survival.

Gwen
(5-11-1921 to 22-9-2011)

You held her hand and stroked her hair
before you lost one of the few;
your mother, friend and cherished dear.

You'll miss her rising from her chair,
the space she filled, the kiss she blew,
to hold her hand and stroke her hair.

Recall her gifts of warmth and cheer,
enduring love that grew and grew
from mother, friend and cherished dear.

You'll see something she used to wear
or catch her scent, a song she knew.
She held your hand and stroked your hair

through all your life, for many years
she brought you up, was there for you;
your mother, friend and cherished dear.

So tell her things you want to share,
she'll hear you still, I'm sure it's true.
You held her hand and stroked her hair;
your mother, friend and cherished dear.

How to Speak to Lions

To address the mighty Simba
you must show profound respect
and whisper admiration
for the mane around his neck.

If he allows you dialogue,
at his savannah gala,
it is wise to carry with you
the leg of an impala.

Beware his muscle-flexing wives
and the game of chase they play.
So talk to not upset him
or from very far away,

or take a slower-running foe,
or learn to speak Swahili:
'Tafadhali hakuna
kusukutua mimi.'

Hygiene

Scrub my face
scour tooth and nail and heel
wash
each niche and splash
soapy water over body
so I'm crisp and
clean.
Immerse me in wholesome
bathing place.

Freshly bathed
made pure and fit for God.
Dress.
Immaculate
white cotton and delicate silk
soft against skin.
Brush
gleaming hair in braid and
go get laid.

Instinct

The naive monitor mirrors my face.
My sly avatar, fast and lean,
emerges for the chase,
disfigures foes across the screen;
the fantastic, majestic, faerie queen.
I seek a mate in halls of fame,
a gallant prince - unseen.
But artful players are hard to claim.
I settle for a mortal man in Nature's game.

John & Gwen

While pain tried to bar their way,
Solent breezes seemed to say,
'Touch not these but pass them by –
heaven bound let loved ones fly.'

In death our hearts renew their youth
lightened of life that pain confines,
their silent rest unveils the truth,
recalling bliss that love enshrines.

The Journey of the Ants

The balcony at Coral Beach
with table, pair of chairs and ants,
where we have brought a plainer lunch
and sit amongst the ochre plants.

Before we've done the ants make trail,
in twos and threes, along the rail.
They route to crumbs and find the strings
of 'nana skins and sweeter things.

We lose a half of cheesy puff
and watch the foragers relate
its whereabouts, while greeting mates,
with pincers full of orange stuff.

A negro hero tightly clings
to fallen friend; an end that brings
renewing feast; that's nature's grail:
no thing is waste while ants prevail.

In pairs, with sun dark skin, we dance;
in nuclear threes we march and munch
the rich delights that Cyprus grants
but fail to learn what insects teach.

The Last Room

Bonding with the welder to make the last room:
two men high, three men long; charged alone*.
The scent of brimstone acetylene sparks roam
across the factory floor, to meet the maker's deadline.

Two men high, three men long; each charged alone.
Brick upon refractory brick along the steel cells
across the factory floor; the maker-meeting dead line.
Testing the metal, testing computerized consoles.

Like brick upon refractory brick along the steel cells
piled in redundant rows. To ponder what remains,
testing your mettle, testing your ability to console
a wife and children, left without the means.

Piled in redundant rows to ponder what remains
of a working life, gone up in smoke – a pyre.
The wife and children; left without the means
if you don't survive and find a way out of despair.

A working life gone up in smoke – a pyre
of reminiscent brimstone acetylene. Thoughts roam
if you don't survive and find a way out of despair:
try bonding with the welder who made the last room.

*charged alone: crematorium furnaces are 'charged' with a single
body and its coffin.*

34

Lawnmower

The gift was a napalm lawnmower.
At first its pristine blades
pummelled the grass,
pushing it North and South
in regimented stripes.
The battle progressed against dandelions
consuming his time in earth.

Like a P.O.W. escaping to the park,
he saw wild grass splattered with poppies
and longed to let his garden explode.

Lazy Day at the Fete

Despite the rain there is a glimmer
of hope to stop us being glummer.
So stow the stew pots' winter simmer.
Get ready to succumb to summer

Don't paint the fence or clear the gutter,
don't mow all day or call the plumber,
drag the golfer from his putter.
Get ready to succumb to summer.

Prepare the scones, the cream and butter,
the stalls of cakes and apple crumble,
the well thumbed books and other clutter,
and pasting tables full of jumble.

And feted is the Morris mummer,
the jingling bells and tambour drummer,
the thwack of sticks to scare all-comers.
Get ready to succumb to summer.

See fairy wings near lilac flutter,
hear buzzing of the hedgerow hummer
and thrumming midges fuzzy mutter.
Get ready to succumb to summer.

Leviathan

The harbour's ripple-blown surface is home
to majestic whale-hulls. From prow to aft
made good by architect-craft's hard labour;
fully tracing all long-past's tragic wrecks
and loan task-graft skills to chasing skipper.

A runnel of flesh-sacs bring dead torches;
swarm, fingering the vertigo rigging;
engrave their blood in the sea-vat brickwork;
leave scrape-skin on malingering tarmac;
scorch the rats out of the flood-up tunnels.

Sparks glint in the pent-up deck then vanish.
Cod-acetylene leaks stink up the wharf;
can't prevent the bold-explode cap-gashing,
swarf-shrapnel threshing welders in the hold.
No gifts for them sod-worth the working stint.

Lord Rooker's Requiem

I saw a bee in winter. Velvet fleece
of sun and midnight keeps him warm. Yet, strange
no clover patch or summer field of wheat
entice. He's unaware of climate change.

The mobiles' waves disorient his head.
His hive is void by mites and throng disease
and disappeared through pesticidal spread.
This worker thrums a requiem for bees.

From tiny loss, the chaos starts a chain;
The knell of death for flora, vetch and grain.
As immigrant and *Bombus* breeds compete,
leaves Sichuan girls to pollinate by hand.
Inter our heads as soil transforms to sand.
A glass of mead will never taste as sweet.

Lord Rooker – 2007 food-and-farming minister predicted the
extinction of the honeybee by 2017.

Lounge

Lounge is an aptly designated room.
Like Van Gogh's napping peasants' bed of corn
on softly comfy sofas we succumb;
we rest and snooze away when we are worn.
The carpet, made from Wilton weavers' loom,
has squares that decorate it like mosaics
in Mediterranean bistros where some
are hung with prow-framed sentimental pics.

I love this cosy amber coloured womb;
its shelves of films from Disney and from Potter.
Relax, divest your care and hurry home
to warm yourself and bathe in terracotta.
This haven needs no better made example:
Irene, our cat, who treats it like her temple.

Man and Machine

It's no good moping about my thinning hair –
This problem's faced by half the human race.
Paranoia reigns and the sentence feels harsh,
unfair that one once handsome is caught red-
handed dyeing, looking for a dream, coming
up with the flimsy palliate sports car.

My heap's waiting for a service at the car
showroom. The cocky salesman, all slick hair
and younger than my toothbrush, is coming
over like a Viagra flash. A racing
commentary ensues, faster than red
adrenaline. Wide-boy, to be bluntly harsh.

His rhetoric could charm my wife, who speaks harsh
words; begrudging my purchase of a new car.
I'm wary when her flushing cheeks grow red
with rage and rant, fuel to the flaming hair.
Horse power won't appease this two-horse race
I need a ploy, a cunning way for coming

up with a solution. I see her coming
around to my way of thinking, less harsh
more purring caress, out of the rat race;
a vacation in the seductive car.
She can relish the winding roads, the hair-
pin bends, glide the beast, thrusting vibrant red.

Glibly as a matador I wave the red
rag to the bullish cow, see her coming
at me full charge, quickening the hair-
raising spectacle of her thinning harsh
lips, smiling. My sense, blinded by the car,
confident that I have made her heart race

as fast as mine. Invigorating racy
thoughts to rekindle romance in harlot red
lace. On tenterhooks I let her drive the car.
Astounded that I didn't see it coming,
crushing my fantasy, fumbling and the harsh
crunch of gears. Her: vapid, not turning a hair.

She tucked her hair behind her ear and read
the riot act. I braced against the coming
fight. The bitter truth is harsh. I sold the car.

Mobile Stones

We took bubblegum pink nets and lines
with net bags holding bait to tangle claws
so the crabs could not release and splash home.
Lucy and Ellen wanted to fish from the pontoon;
to trail their toes in the water while we waited.
The bacon worked a treat.
We captured more than would fit comfortably
in the bucket, refilled it three times.
Each time the crabs scuttled back to the estuary,
their pincers held high like pugilists,
their behinds wedged between the planks.
Lucy was bravest and picked one up
squealing as its cocktail stick legs pushed,
prickled her fingers; trying to escape.
We examined the bodies in the bucket; a stream
of bubbles surfaced, showing the crushees lived;
big ones still shovelling fat into mandibles.
Picking one up, I felt the gritty exterior,
its barnacled back; rough to the touch. Flailing limbs
made me drop the sea stone, revealing its belly
of breast plate muscle coloured bright citrus,
orange and lime shreds under its mud-coloured
shell; rock-hard to dissuade the circling gulls.

Monitor

See it?
There. A skull,
a spinal bone atoll,
dark bulbous eyes,
umbilical tail.
The mottled, striated bands,
 in a sonic sweep, quiver across
  denary magnification of the alien;
  its inchoate limbs, a claw like fist
  suckled, ready when the parasite
 emerges. The hatchling floating
in mucus. We search the screen
for a scaly, buckled creature;
the fluttering heart pulse
 confirming life.
 Fascinating,
 like poking
 a stick at
 a basking
 lizard.

Motherhood is a Rhinoceros

It's grey;
you find it in the background of pictures.
It's obvious;
you would know when it's in a room.
It's unshakeable;
always strong because of its stature.
It's protective;
you wouldn't want to face an angry one.

Mrs Meacher

trying to pilot her generous hips
between rows of exam desks,
brushes neon crayons to the floor.

An electric crackle ripples
through the herd of students,
each face turns to the noise.

Her grimace, a smile - lizard's feather
rare, makes three hundred heads
dip to their maths paper,

Thirty faces per class, thirty years
of lame excuses, v-signs, poison pens
all for an apology of a pension.

Rumour nips the staff room banter,
blighted by some politician's angle
to extend her child bearing years.

My Foolish Lover Gave Me Chocolates

Open the packaged ballotin of pralines.
The Mayan morsels moisten salvation;
inhale aromatic mocha bicerin;
roll them around; andante rotation.
Each sweet, a nibbled taste of bitter bean,
contains delicious noisettes that I need.
A shot of luscious cinnamon with caffeine;
this ganache yields the energy for greed.

I'm rapt unwrapping foil off rose raspberry,
smothered in darkest chocolate layered crumb.
The dulcet liqueur cups a glacé cherry
with sticky fingers and with sucky thumb;
A fantasy of cocoa dusted fruit.
I consummate this nuptial substitute.

The New Zoo

It was opening day at the new zoo
and the head keeper addressed the men of
the green team; his debut crew. Keep your eyes
out for the arrival of the vet who
was due to rate the pen of the greater
kudu. The vet said the herd grew too fast
and would have to be moved soon. Then he wiped
a glob of gnu goo off his arm as
he noticed the brilliant blue hue of
a peacock's tail fan. Spoke on cue, 'Phew! I'm
hot and thirsty for a true brew of tea
and two choux,' famished, watching the panda
munching its bamboo chew. After drinking
his cuppa he made his way to the loo
queue, which was long. He returned to the main
office via the Peru View beside
the paddock of the Chilean pudu;
near the path leading through to the petting
yard where a few ewes had wandered into
a heap of kangaroo poo. The vet said
he'd pursue clues to find how this mix-up
occurred. The culprit cried and wailed, 'boo-hoo!'
but threatened the vet with Voodoo. He missed
but the spell caught the boss who said, 'Oh-oh'

Pentad

Their bodies were heavy.
Hauled into my car boot,
hefted to the kitchen table.
Each of five swollen brutes
dismembered on marble.

Slicing caps at an angle,
scooped out ice-cold brain;
distended threads of pulp.
Threshing knife to mangle,
gouging innards clean.

With serrated blade of metal
I carved scars through the skin,
threw eyes to piles of gore,
scraped canines, jagged jaws;
fingers bore the fleshy stain.

Matching caps to heads
I washed off the limpet caul.
In the gloom of the shed
a fire in each hollow skull
leaked shadows on the wall.

I moved them to the garden;
a show to freak out children.
Checking later in the night
a snail clung to one cheek,
peeked into the demon's eye.

Picking My Nose

My Mum took me back to the clinic,
berated the clones picked to mimic;
the genome designer;
the codon refiner;
rejected the slur she's a finick.

My eyes are the colour she wanted,
my brain is the sort that she flaunted.
Each piece from the brochure
is here, but there's no cure,
'cos Nature prevailed – so I'm taunted.

The nurse showed the waiver so smugly,
my Mum was annoyed that I'm ugly,
mutational guano;
a throw back Cyrano.
I'm me and I wish she would hug me.

Proud

We tuck away our tempting treasure
reserved for subtle, secret pleasure,
encased and chaste and out of sight;
a cavern rich with pure delight.

For years of prudish legacy,
or fear of what's above the knee,
No hillside giant celebrates;
No totem bowl to say 'That's great.'

Synchro swimmers, hurdle jumpers,
divers, runners, pedal pumpers
gymnasts, vaulters, volley players
wearing thinnest lycra layers
can show us proudly how they're maid
and win Olympic accolades.

30th Olympiad, London 2012

Rose

Rose cleans the office every working day.
Her duster whisks and Henry Hoover hums,
ensures the bin contents are thrown away
and wonders if this work makes her seem dumb.

The clever people working here say 'hi'
but do so out of custom not for care.
Their classy cars are more than she could buy;
their formal suits make dowdy what she wears.

A quiet tea-break sees her muse about
the life that might be hers with men like this;
the wealth that comes with exercising clout
and taking what you want with just one kiss.

She should have known 'her beauty' was a con.
Illicit love was all that made him throb.
Too soon his wife returned and Rose was gone
with one result; at least she kept her job.

Rowner in the Rain

The baleful stumps await the season.
Eleven warriors turn up to pitch
their pent up energies on Saturday.

Let loose from their suits,
cops and clerks and motley managers
seek out last year's whites,
shrunken in the wardrobe,
now holding back a surfeit of pies.
They seek out last year's cups
grown faintly green and sour
from the dampness of the last match.
They seek out last year's bats
and retrieve the rusting linseed tin
from the spare room's neglected junk,

Between the Dragon and the bottle bank,
where the junkies' needles glitter,
the umpire cuffs the yob spraying graffiti
before a tea-time bet at Don Simmons.
Play slows while the police separate
brawling women in the pub garden.
Nothing entirely stops play;
not volcano clouds from Iceland,
not for Elvis, Lennon or Jackson,
not the ungentlemanly accusations.
The players, from colts to curmudgeons,

continue to break wind in the slips,
continue their scurrilous brotherhood,
continue even when it's raining.

Sexting

i fink u r wel fit w8ing outside maf
do u want 2 hang wiv me, go 4 piza?
ur braces suit d prpl bands, deyr cute
its gr8 ur frnds all fink im buf.
ur arse is wak, id lv 2 touch ur baps
i dream bout ur hand round my cok
cum bak 2 mine, my rents r out
we can kiss. r u on d pill?

i cant c ur face. it sux you'd sext so harsh
wre not 2 yung…im not…2 fel dis wa
it canes dat you wont go wiv me
am i a freak 4 wntng you, wntng lv?
go wiv ur m8s n laugh at me
lol at dis final txt…when im ded. ☹

Smoke Me

So urgent is your need
      when you crinkle the cellophane undone.
Tissue-smooth skin, tight with weed.
      You select one icosatuplet clone.

Do you think of football plans
      in our seven-six-seven formation?
Slide one out. Defy the ban.
      Curve rubs curve in a sensual motion.

Pressed firmly against your lips
      I smoulder; alive at last and burning.
Kiss my fleshy filter tips.
      I'm heedless that you don't heed my warning.

Snow Castles

Ellen had to be restrained from dashing
out into the garden, changed by flurries
of albino spiders parachuting
softly onto the lawn, shrubs and path.

Agitated she watched each flake gather,
smother the earth in imagination.
I gave permission for gloves and galoshes,
she scurried to stamp footfalls in innocence.

Patches of grass appeared, leading to
a half-finished, headless Frosty. Nearby,
on a once-wooden seat, an icy teddy
perched, silently observing Ellen at play.

Soon she needed implements; the spade,
the anniversary bouquet bucket, now kept
to capture migraine retching, was stuffed
with scoops of snow and stuttered out

castle walls of sawn-off, ice-cream cones.
A second row progressed the pyramid, begun
fanatically, petered as her face flushed;
she shook her arms to fling away the chill.

A lack of ambition, and perhaps frustration
that I wouldn't venture into the cold to help,
to raise the pinnacle. The sullen destruction;
she scattered her creation to cries of 'timber'.

By embers, we stared at decimated mounds.
I told her of a snowfield in the North
where I launched into chest-high ditches,
the frozen walk home with stone mittens.

The Sun on the Other Side

The sun has left traces embedded
in green shrubs and grasses; each cell
of chlorophyll created by her light.

Her passing brings an evening chill
seen as the blooms close. I watch
a foraging hedgehog scratching

at the lawn for worms drawn out
of the dew-moist earth; rainbow snakes
to quench thirst and sate his hunger.

His regular path marked by the spaces
between leaves and turned gravel;
disturbances, the footprints of his spirit

wandering the night when the sun
is in the dreaming, shedding its warmth
where we are given to the land,

to protect its enduring mantle
and leave it safe, unmolested; ready
for the generations that will follow

our songlines, walk the ancient paths;
able to find each pool of reflection
and each rising as the sun returns.

The Time of Your Life

Recall events that beggar all belief -
The facelift and Chanel disguise decay.
With credit cards the change of life is brief.

The claxons at the exit squealing 'thief',
Lynn's pockets full of trinkets from displays,
present events that beggar all belief.

Her lawyer's playing golf - no bail relief.
Detention's harsh; the cell is cold and grey.
A life of credit makes her change her brief.

At court her oath is honest, full of grief.
Observers back her plea of folly; they
recall events that beggar all belief.

A woman in her fifties sits as chief
magistrate. There's a token fine Lynn pays
with credit cards. The change of life is brief.

The H.R. patch in place, Lynn turns a leaf;
to spend less time in jail, in case she may
recall events that beggar all belief.
With credit cards the change of life is brief

Wacko Jacko

25 June 2009. To the tune of Bobby Shafto.

Wacko Jacko passed awa-ay,
they have played his songs all da-ay,
all his fans are in disma-ay.
Bad ole Wacko Jacko.

Wacko Jacko wanted pla-ay;
overnight your kids could sta-ay,
in the morning he would pa-ay.
Bad ole Wacko Jacko.

Wacko Jacko's nose of cla-ay
always falling off his fa-ace,
he turned white but now he's gra-ay.
Bad ole Wacko Jacko.

Wacko Jacko start to pra-ay,
clutch your balls and squeal out he-ey,
moonwalk through the pearly ga-ates.
Bad ole Wacko Jacko.

The Way I Want to Go

Quickly...yes...I want to go...quickly.
No dilatory death, no years of waiting
for a doctor or surgeon to say, 'you are sickly'
or relatives deciding my treatment debating

loudly what's best to be done in my case.
Brow raised in surprise like a sharp frost in May,
at speed, rapidly, at quite a fast pace;
like a gunshot, a blink or a lap dance sashay;

as a victim of fate or unexpected revenge;
stabbed *in flagrante* with carotid blood spilling;
not to linger as long as the stones at Stone Henge.
I'd go to my grave with a heart almost willing.

Bring me wreaths, little poems, but stop your tears flowing,
it may not be soon for my quick-death desire.
I've no idea when but I know where I'm going;
the service will end when Johnny sings *Ring of Fire*

Words Like Needles

Words like needles need to fit
in subtle ways and leave no mark;
to knit a row and patch a split,
words like needles need to fit
where feelings fray, unlit and stark,
pin point a phrase and darn the dark.
Words like needles need to fit
in subtle ways to make their mark.

You Wake

'like a dog, he hunts in dreams'
                    - Alfred Lord Tennyson

In depths of sleep the mysteries unfold.
Things mulled and twined are sorted out
in vivid light and fuelled

by spicy food or cheese; some thing you ate.
The hounds that chase you close and tear -
You wake, but there's no bite.

Another night you swim until you tire.
The beach is where the bedroom sits –
You wake, but there's no shore.

And, driving down a bowling lane, the pins
all chase you. Teeth you've lost return.
You wake, and roll with pains

all down one side and find the sheets are torn.
Then back to hunt the boss's work
and stress on how you'll earn
some luck; so dream until you wake.

Zoo Villanelle

In time we'll see there comes a day
to recognise the loss we feel
when every person thinks this way;

the price of entry that we pay
and funds for sponsorship appeal.
In time we'll see there comes a day

to save all species poachers slay
with breeding stock and vets who heal
when every person thinks this way.

The joy of watching beasts at play;
no picture book; this all is real.
It's time to see and spend the day

and think of steak while haunches sway.
Our beastly instincts can't conceal
that every person thinks this way.

But see the signs on cages say
'Don't feed or you'll become the meal.'
In time we'll see there comes the day
that every creature thinks this way.